Toledo
The Imperial City

Seen from the *Carretera del Valle*, the city seems to defy the shadows of twilight, entrenching itself in the "Tagus loop", whose waters reflect and multiply the city lights.

Edited by:
Thema, Equipo Editorial, S.A.

Translated by:
Carole Patton

Photography by:
Frederic Camallonga and Domi Mora
For the corresponding subject:
© Monasterio de San Juan de los Reyes.
Toledo. Spain

© SUSAETA EDICIONES S.A.
Campezo, s/n
28022 – Madrid
Tel.: 913 009 100
Fax: 913 009 118

This extraordinary panoramic view of Toledo from the other side of the River Tagus gives us a pretty good idea of the city's exceptional emplacement.

Contents

	Cradle of Charm and Understanding	11
	At the Foot of the Alcázar	27
	The Cathedral	39
	Bridges	51
	Churches and Hospitals	59
	Synagogues and Mosques	73
	Streets with History	79
	Swords and Marzipan	89

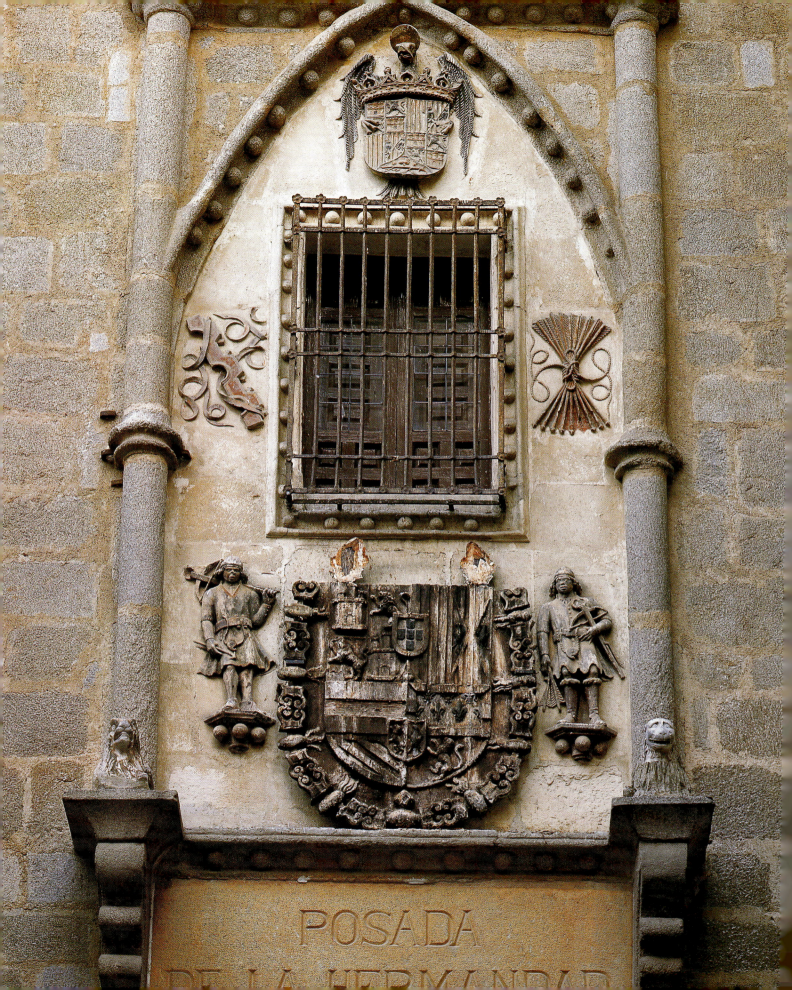

The *Posada de la Hermandad* was one of the Toledan inns for "important persons" as the writer Miguel de Cervantes states in *La ilustre fregona*, one of his famous *Novelas ejemplares*.

Toledo
The Imperial City

The people of Toledo
Are affable, discreet, honourable,
Charitable, pious,
More than I can say [...]
Lope de Vega («Hamete de Toledo»)

Frontiers
The nature of art shows the ambiguous limit between light and shade.

Moorish Art
The fine, subtle, Moorish art of stuccowork shapes the material into forms of nature.

Order
The complex pattern on the borders describes the order of a harmonious cultural universe.

Writing
Cufic writing at the service of celestial poetry adorning the city of men.

Christian
Castilian canons seek their line on the walls of the Christian temple.

Shadows
Christian hands project their shadows over the walls of the temple of the Lord.

From the high walls of the *Alcázar* our eyes scan the city rooftops as far as the *Puerta de la Bisagra* and the square tower of the Mudéjar church of *Santiago del Arrabal*.

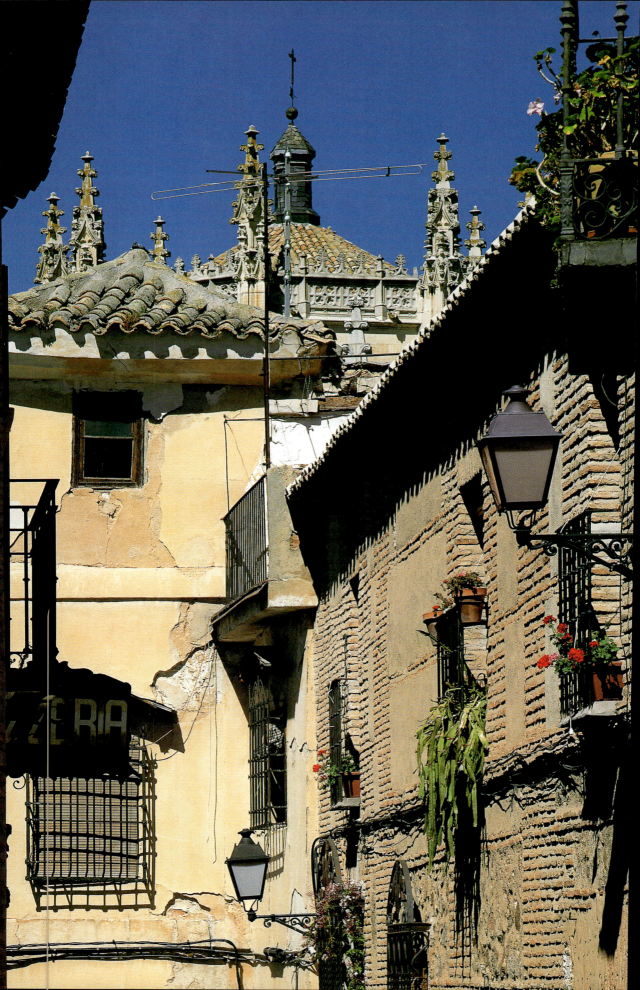

Toledo

The Imperial City

CRADLE OF CHARM AND UNDERSTANDING
In the "Tagus Loop"

On the plateau of Castile, in the area between La Sagra and the Mesa de Ocaña, where the River Tagus loops around a granite hill, the so-called *torno del Tajo* ("the Tagus Loop"), lies the place that was chosen by primitive Iberian tribes to settle.

In time, *carpetanos* turned the settlement into a fortified town, whose strategic location attracted the Romans, as witnessed by Titus Livius. After some resistance, Marcus Fulvius Nobilior conquered the town in 192 B.C. and named it *Toletum*. Converted into a strategic point on the road that joined *Emerita* (Merida) and *Caesaraugusta*

Street
Chiaroscuros mark the geometry of a city that grew in a climate of tolerance and respect.

Alcázar
The austere Renaissance style imposes its harmonic lines, outlining one of the most emblematic buildings in the history of Toledo. Its stones have withstood fire and war.

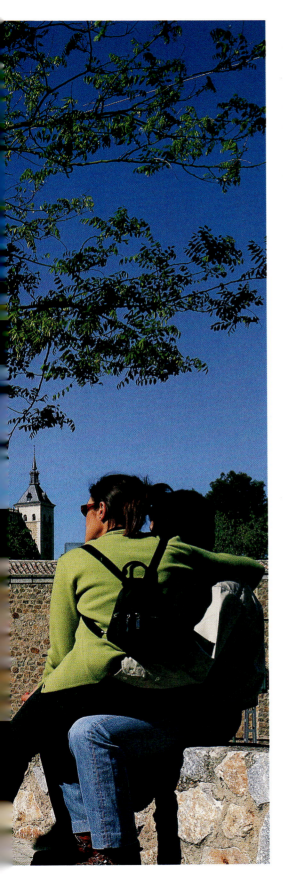

Castle of San Servando
Ancient fortress that formed part of Toledo's defensive system. Its walls and tower are from the end of the 14th century. Lope de Vega tells us how duels were fought beneath its walls.

Afuera Hospital
The Archbishop of Toledo, Juan Pardo de Tavera, Inquisitor and Member of the Royal Council, ordered this Renaissance-style building to be constructed.

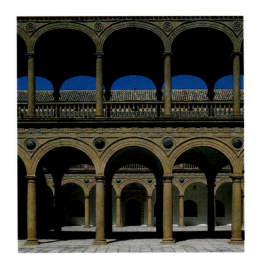

(Zaragoza), the town was then fortified, its walls overlooking the river and the vast plains on which villas and olive groves soon started to spring up. The *Alcántara* bridge, an aqueduct, a circus, walls and numerous temples and civil constructions were also important features of the Roman town.

The City of Seven Hills

The expansion of Christianism within the imperial frontiers was especially important for Toledo. The Christians are responsible for the greatness of its origins and the spreading of various legends, a characteristic that went on for centuries, reaching its highest point during the 16th century. This was when Father Jerónimo de la Higuera "invented" seven hills to compare it with Rome, from the four on which the city is built. However, the splendour of Toledo is not only due to these intentions of mythifying its origins and foundation, but to the ways and deeds of its inhabitants. Already back in Roman times, an important iron industry had been developped, the town also having been granted the right to coin money. Towards the 4th century, now an episcopal seat, Barbarian invasions led the Hispano-Romans to further fortifying the town walls. But nothing could be done to stop the process of the breaking up of the empire, and Franks, Alans and Goths successively conquered the town.

Atanagild the Goth understood

Mudéjar Art
Magnificent 14th-century room, whose finely stuccoed walls display Koranic, Hebrew and Christian verses, complementing the ceramic objects, tiles and wooden craftwork.

The Moor's Workshop
Built in 1366 by Moorish architects who lived among the Christians. It belonged to the Order of Alcántara, which respected the Hebrew writing that can be seen on the top cornice.

the strategic location of Toledo and set up court there in the 6th century. Leovigild made it the capital of his kingdom, giving it the name of the town, his son Recared confirming this decision in 587. From that time on, builders, silversmiths, goldsmiths, potters and artists contributed to the magnificence of the "royal city". The Goths chose Toledo as their episcopal seat where they held important councils dealing with the heavenly and earthly matters that concerned the Church in those days. From this period are the remains of the great wall built under the orders of King Wamba, the *Cristo de la Luz Hermitage*, where councils were held, as well as the items on display at the Visigothic Culture and Councils Museum, housed in the Church of *San Román*.

Tolerant Tolaitola

In 711, Toledo fell into the hands of the Moors, and remained under their control until 1085, when it was reconquered again by the Christians, led by the Castilian King Alfonso IV.

During their rule of more than three centuries, the Moors changed the appearance of the town that was on the edge of Al-Andalus. In the days of the Caliphate of Córdoba, *Tolaitola*, as it was called by the Moors, reached its heyday, having a population of nearly 40,000 inhabitants and being an important centre of artisans and sword manufacturing. The swords from Toledo, with their steel cooled down in the waters of the Tagus and their damascene hilts and pommels, were well-renowned on both sides of the frontier.

On the fall of the Caliphate, Toledo achieved its independence as a taifa kingdom, which lasted until Christian reconquest.

Apart from the impressive *Alcázar* (Moorish palace), built on the ruins of the Romano-Visigothic fortress, the Moors left us such beautiful monuments as the *mezquitas* (mosques) of *Bib Mardum* and *Las Tornerías*, the baths located on *Calle del Ángel* and *Calle del Pozo* and the gates *Puerta Vieja de la Bisagra* and *Puerta del Sol*. But the most important legacy left by the Moors was the climate of harmony reflected in the fluid relationship amongst Muslims, Jews and Christians.

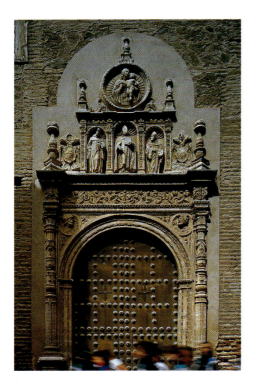

Church of San Clemente
Baroque forms determine the lines, contours, columns and sculptures of the austere and elegant façade of the Church of *San Clemente*. The lavishness of its ornamentation corresponds to the power of the Church in the Spanish empire.

Town Hall
Jorge Manuel Theotokopoulos used the Renaissance designs of the architect Juan de Herrerra to finish, between 1613 and 1619, the sturdy building of the Town Hall, whose elegance is highlighted in this night view.

King of Three Religions

The spirit of tolerance that prevailed as a characteristic of the city was assumed by the first Christian kings of Toledo. The best example of this was Alfonso X, "the Wise One", who liked to be known as the "king of the three religions". Thanks to him, the most important centre of European learning of the Middle Ages was established, the *Escuela de Traductores de Toledo* (Translators' School of Toledo). Here, scholars belonging to different cultures translated ancient works from the most varied of sources into Castilian Spanish, thus reestablishing the historical continuity of scientific and artistic learning, and contributing to the determination of Spanish literary prose.

In this climate of harmony, the Jewish community achieved great importance, its contribution being decisive to the magnification and embellishment of Toledo. Monumental remains left to us by the Jews are the synagogues of *Santa María la Blanca* and *El Tránsito*, located in the old Jewish quarter.

The arrival of the 15th century, with the reign of the Catholic Monarchs, meant a point of inflection in the fluid relationship among religious communities. Their Christian policy was based on dogmatism and intolerance, introducing, in 1478, the Sacred Office of the Holy Inquisition that focused its attention especially on suspicious Jew converts.

In 1492, the persecution of the

Cava Palace

After Toledo was reconquered by Christian armies, the austere and sober lines of Castilian architecture started to gain ground in the town. Nobles belonging to diverse military and religious orders displayed their power and strength by building palaces that were authentic fortresses and which, in a way, formed part of the town's defensive system. The Gothic Palace of *Los duques de Maqueda* or *La Cava,* with its battlemented walls, is a perfect example of the new religious order.

Fuensalida Palace
Muslim, Hebrew and Christian communities. In this sense, one of the most representative civil constructions of Muslim architects and craftsmen among Christians is the Palace of *Fuensalida*. Here Gothic building ideas blend perfectly with the mudéjar ornamentation inside.

A Real Museum

When El Greco settled in Toledo, he lived in this typical house, where he would die in 1614. Careful reconstruction and refurbishment have resulted in this House-Museum where one may admire works by the artist and his disciples, as well as objects belonging to Toledo's classic period.

The Burial of the Count of Orgaz

In this splendid painting by El Greco, which can be found in the Church of *Santo Tomé*, there is a clear limit between the heavenly and the earthly, the two different atmospheres being well-defined. It is a fine example of the artist's mastery of composition. Toledo had profoundly impressed the artist, who knew how to portray the impact the place had had on him.

Jews came to its height with the massive expulsion of Spanish Jews, and, ten years later, all non converts were ordered to leave the domains of Castile. All this brought terrible consequences upon the town, whose arts and industries were paralysed, thus putting an end to its age of splendour, leaving us with its monumentality and character of an imperial city.

El Greco

During the 16th century, Toledo was the strongest focus of resistance to the imperial policies of Carlos V. In fact, it was one of the first towns to revolt and is where the so-called "Communities War" began, being the hometown of some of its main leaders, for example Juan de Padilla, whose widow, María Pacheco, after her husband's execution, headed the Toledan resistance for a further few months.

However, in spite of this tense atmosphere, an event occurred in the town which would be decisive for Spanish art. In 1577, Domenikos Theotokopoulos, better known as El Greco ("The Greek") arrived in Toledo to stay. As Julio Caro Baroja so rightly wrote, "El Greco and Toledo fit and complement each other." During that year, El Greco painted the altarpiece of *Santo Domingo el Antiguo* monastery, the retable having since been divided up, and where, in one of its chapels, his mortal remains can be found, as well as the famous painting "The Spoliation of Christ" in the Cathedral. From that moment on, El Greco started feeling identified with the town, going through a process of "hispanisation" as some have said, which resulted in some of the most emblematic paintings of 16th –century Spain. Converted into a "Spaniard from Toledo" who knew how to transmit that oriental, or should we say Byzantine, mystical spirit in his paintings, El Greco succeeded, like no other, in portraying and reflecting the genuine Toledan society of the times of Felipe II. This artist found the most representative models for his paintings from among the principal inhabitants of the town, as can be seen in his masterpiece "The Burial of the Count of Orgaz", in which he and his son, Jorge Manuel, are also represented. The spirituality

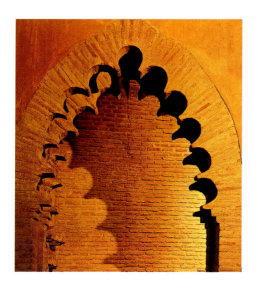

Church of San Román
Detail of the lines of mudéjar inspiration that characterise the style of the Church of *San Román*.

Stone Sentinels
The Gothic spires of the Convent of *San Juan de Reyes* seem to protect Christian peace from an invisible threat. It is the second most important Catholic construction in Toledo built on the orders of the Catholic Monarchs.

that dramatizes the scenes and the anxiety reflected by the expressions on the faces of nobles and Apostles, correspond to the atmosphere of an age dominated by the morals of the Counter Reformation.

It can be said that not only did El Greco succeed in settling down perfectly well in Toledo, but also in many of his paintings we can sense the feeling he held towards his town of adoption, where he had arrived a stranger, with practically no knowledge of the language, and where he remained until his death.

Toledan Religiousness

The religiousness of the days of Felipe II that El Greco knew how to reflect so well in the "heavy" atmosphere of his paintings, in the austerity of his figures and in the distressed look on the faces of his characters, corresponded to the rituals of the Church. Holy Week, with its "Silence" procession, together with Corpus Christi reflect the profound religious sentiment of the inhabitants of this city. For the Corpus procession, the streets of Toledo are decked out with tapestries, carpets and awnings hanging from the balconies, and the ground is strewn with aromatic herbs such as thyme, rosemary and lavender. A float, with carvings made by Bernardo de Miquélez in 1781, carrying the splendid 16th –century Gothic Monstrance, made by Enrique Arfe on the orders of Cardenal Cisneros, is carried out of the Cathedral.

Panoramic View of Toledo
From the *Parador Conde de Orgaz*, located in the area known as *Cerro del Emperador* (The Emperor's Hill), it is possible to enjoy some magnificent views of Toledo, a city which has been declared a World Heritage Site.

The Tagus "Loop"
The "loop" encircles the hill and seems to highlight the town with its ring of water and its aspiration to emulate Rome, lying on the seven hills imagined by the Jesuit Román de la Higuera. The Cathedral, the *Alcázar* and other emblematic buildings stand out.

Also Gothic is the monstrance inside, made from the first gold and silver brought back from America.

From Partridge to Marzipan

The monumental city of Toledo, a World Heritage listed site, has a very old gastronomical tradition. Located between plains and mountains, it has developed a sober and wholesome cuisine, in which local produce and game are especially present. The marinade technique is traditionally Arab, referred to as *sakkab* in "Arabian Nights", used for preparing dishes of partridge or hare, amongst others. A typical Toledan dish is partridge *a la toledana*, cooked slowly and praised by the Infante Don Juan Manuel in his *Enxiemplos* and Cervantes through words spoken by Don Quixote. Another traditional dish is partridge cooked with beans or the well-renowned *cochifrito* –a stew of lamb cooked with tomatoes, egg, saffron and white wine, which renders tribute to shepherding back in the times of the *mesta* [medieval association of shepherds].

However, the one thing the Toledans are really proud of is their marzipan, famous far beyond the bridges spanning the River Tagus. Folklore has it that it was invented by ingenious Moorish cooks during the siege of Toledo by the troops of Alfonso VI. Seemingly, in order to save the inhabitants from starvation, these Moorish women decided to make a purée of almonds and sugar, which they shaped into little buns and baked in the oven. So simple and so exquisite is marzipan.

So, we can see that Toledo has many things that make it unique and admirable, as the poet Rilke expressed. It is said that, after attending one of the spiritualist gatherings of Marie Thurn Taxis, the poet was visited by a spirit who advised him to travel to Toledo, stand under a bridge and sing. However, it was not the magic of the spirit that bewitched him, but the charm of the city. "I could never explain to you in words, my dear friend, (it is the work of angels when helping man ...) They say that God, on the fourth day, took the Sun and placed it right above Toledo", wrote the poet, full of admiration, to the German princess.

At the Foot of the Alcázar

The Alcázar. Its origin goes back to the days of the Romans, who had built it over Iberian fortifications. It is certainly the most representative building of Toledo and its walls keep the historical legacy of the city. When Alfonso VI conquered the town, he ordered his residence to be installed here and, according to tradition, appointed Rodrigo Díaz de Vivar, *El Cid*, as Governor of the castle. Its Renaissance look is work of Carlos V and Felipe II.

Renaissance Monument.
Formerly strengthened by the Visigoths, the Moors turned it into an almost inexpugnable stronghold, passing into history as the *Alcázar*, the Spanish form of the Arabic term *al-qasr*, meaning "castle" or "fortress".
The splendid emplacement of the fortress led the Castilian king to take up residence there, but it was not until the arrival of Carlos V in the 16th century that the palace was built. Entrusted with the works was the Toledan Alonso de Covarrubias, under orders of Prince Felipe (the future Felipe II). The Renaissance appearance of its harmonious façades belong to this period. In particular, the eastern and western sides were given openings without lintels for the basements; flat-arched windows with small roofs and acroters or pedestals on the first floor; flat-arched windows with a triangular fronton adorned with heads on the second, and twice as many flat-arched windows on the top floor. The northern façade was adapted to the horizontality of the walls, which gave it the look of a Renaissance mansion, highlighted by the superb portal, work of Enrique Egas. The southern façade, belonging to the days of Felipe II, was drawn up by Juan de Herrera, who also designed the splendid staircase inside, the work being carried out by Jerónimo Gili.

At the Foot

of the Alcázar

At the Foot of the Alcázar

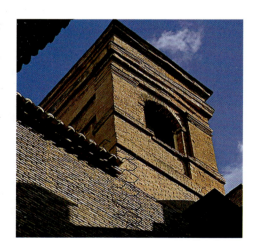

Puerta del Cambrón. The numerous gates appearing every now and again along the sometimes invisible concentric walls tell us about the life and customs of a city marked by the age-old war between Moors and Christians. The Cambrón Gate, seemingly of Visigothic origin, from the days of King Wamba, was one of the small entrances and exits for artisans through one of the circles of walls built by the Moors. According to Rodrigo Amador de los Ríos, the Moorish system of walls had three enclosures with special gates for the use of different artisans. Seemingly, the *Puerta del Cambrón* was a major gate, although in the 19th century it was considered a minor one. In 1576, during the reign of Felipe II, the *Corregidor* Juan Gutiérrez Tello ordered its restoration in an elegant Renaissance style, finishing it off with two towers.

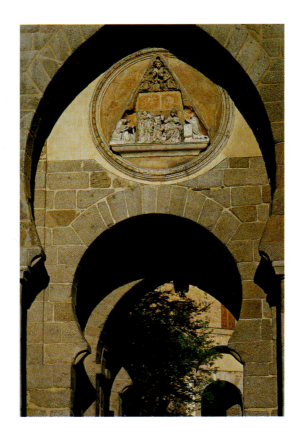

Monumental Puerta del Sol. Many are the legends about the walls and gates of the fortified enclosure of Toledo. The *Puerta del Sol* ("The Sun Gate") is said to be of Roman origin and legend has it that there is a sarcophagus of the early Christians inside. It is also said that it was the most important gate in the days of Wamba, but there are others who claim it to be the work of Archbishop Pedro Tenorio in the 14th century, who made it a monument of mozarabic art, designing it as a triumphal arch.

At the Foot of the Alcázar

Puerta de Alfonso VI. This gate is in fact that of *La Bisagra Vieja*. ("The Old Bisagra Gate") The old "gateway to the countryside" was built during an extension of the fortifications when Toledo was a *taifa* kingdom. Its design is clearly military and it is said that it was through here that the Castilian king entered the supposedly inexpugnable city, with the help of Toledan mozárabes. Alfonso VI knew how to make the most of the help requested by Al-Qadir, the King of Toledo, to enter the city and conquer the kingdom by capitulations.

At the Foot

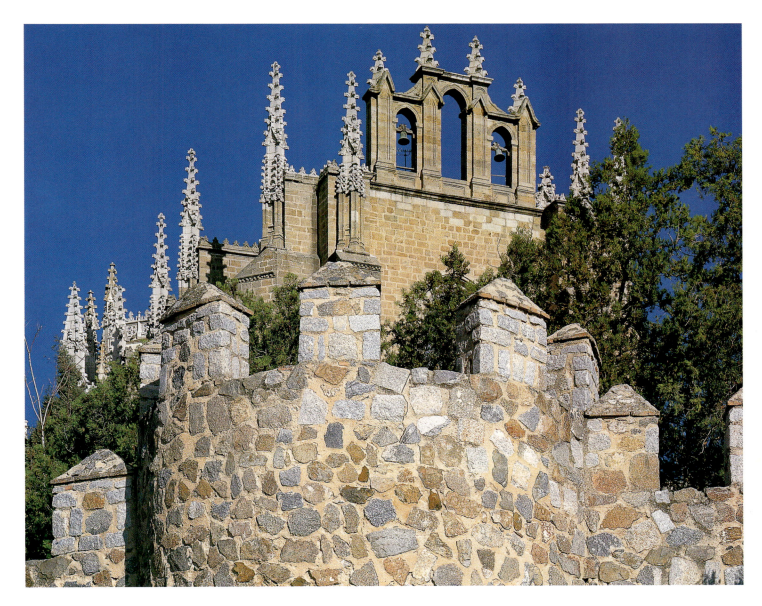

Battlements and Spires. A few metres away from the Bridge of *San Martín*, and supported by the battlemented walls which delimit the fortified enclosure on the side of the river, is the Monastery of *San Juan de los Reyes*. Just like prickly ears of wheat, its spires flank the bell gable of the Gothic monastery which the Catholic Monarchs ordered to be built to commemorate the victory over the Portuguese that put an end to *La Beltraneja*'s aspirations to the throne. The monastery represents the arrival of Christian art in a city dominated by Muslim tendencies.

of the Alcázar

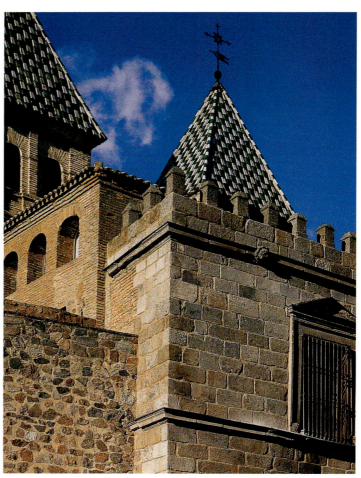

Puerta de la Bisagra and Santiago del Arrabal. From the top of the Mudéjar bell tower of the Church of *Santiago del Arrabal*, whose tower dates back to the 12th century, there is a splendid view of the *Puerta Nueva de la Bisagra* ("The New Bisagra Gate"). It is the most impressive of Toledo's nine gates and was built in 1550, in honour of Carlos V. This explains its Renaissance look and the imperial coat-of-arms on the façade. Until the 18th century the Bisagra Gate used to close at night-time.

At the Foot of the Alcázar

The Cathedral

Monument of Christianity. Toledo Cathedral synthesises the city's religious history and the universal character of faith of those who ordered its construction. For a long time it was known as "the Giant", being one of the five largest cathedrals in the world. It is also important due to the artistic and liturgical treasures that it houses, such as El Greco's famous painting "Spoliation of Christ", the *Transparente* by Narciso Tomé or the famous Monstrance by Enrique de Arfe.

The Cathedral

Bell Tower. The monumental bell tower, built at the end of the 16th century, towers 90 metres above the roofs of the city. It is said that when its largest bell, known as *la Gorda* ("The Fat One") rang out for the first time, all the windows in Toledo were shattered. This is where the famous monstrance is kept.

Puerta de los Leones. "The Lion Door" is a side entrance that leads into the southern arm of the transept and the Chapter House. Its façade was built at the end of the 15th century by Annequin Egas, who gave it its rich adornment.

Cathedral Surroundings. Near the cathedral, people stroll the streets of old Toledo, visiting the traces of history that are to be found in this artistic and monumental city.

The Cathedral

By Night. It is said that Alfonso VI promised Ulema Abu Walid that, in spite of it being an old Christian temple, he would respect the mosque as a place of worship. But, in his absence, Queen Constanza and Archbishop Bernardo took it by storm and placed a bell in the minaret.

By Day. When Alfonso VI returned to Toledo, he punished those who had broken his promise and gave the temple back to the Muslims. Touched by this, Abu Walid handed the mosque over to the Christians. That was why his figure was sculpted between angels.

The "Transparente". For centuries, the best and most important sculptors, wood carvers and religious image makers took part in the Cathedral works. The impressive sculpture known as the *Transparente* (left) was carried out by Narciso Tomé and his sons between 1729 and 1732. This marble Baroque masterpiece is located in the middle of the ambulatory, creating an original dramatic effect in comparison to the Gothic serenity. Maybe this is highlighted by the ray of heavenly light that comes from the skylight in the apse and which reaches the sanctuary.

Main Aisle and Retrochoir. Toledo cathedral has five aisles. The main aisle is covered by impressive ribbed vaults supported on high Gothic columns, whose simplicity of line contrast greatly with the lavish decoration of the retrochoir.

The Cathedral

The Cathedral

Chapter House. Designed and carried out by Enrique Egas and Pedro Gumiel between 1504 and 1512, this work is a perfect blend of the mudéjar and Renaissance styles. Especially outstanding are the paintings by Juan de Borgoña and the splendid coffered ceiling, with richly decorated friezes.

Toledo Cathedral was founded by Saint Eugene in the 6th century in the days of Recared. The Moors then converted it into a mosque and Alfonso VI gave it back its Christian character. In 1226, Fernando III ordered its demolition and later reconstruction. (Following two pages.)

Bridges

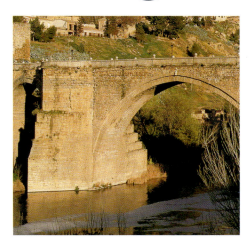

Crossing the Tagus. The bridges spanning the river were formerly part of the defensive system of the most inexpugnable Spanish town. Romans, Visigoths, Moors and Castilians used them as bulwarks that no army could pass without the consent of its inhabitants. Historical bridges are those of *San Martín*, dating from the 13th and 16th centuries, and *Alcántara*, meaning "the bridge" in Arabic, located opposite King Wamba's historical gate.

Bridges

Bridge of San Martín. For centuries, this was one of the main entrances to the city. Located on the west, it was an important part of Toledo's defences. In 1203, the bridge near the *Baño de la Cava* was swept away by floods, and another one was built. In the 14th century, during the civil war between Pedro I and Enrique de Trastámara, the bridge was partly destroyed. Therefore, for some time, the *Alcántara* Bridge was mostly used for crossing the river. On the death of Pedro I, "the Cruel One", Archbishop Pedro Tenorio ordered its restoration. However, the bridge we see today corresponds to 17th —century reforms.

Bridge over the River Tagus. Today's bridge of *San Martín* (left), in spite of the reforms, is a Gothic construction with mudéjar elements of great sobriety and beauty. Flanked by two towers and their corresponding gates, it was joined to the western part of the walls, not very far from *San Juan de los Reyes* Monastery, whose battlements and spires can be seen from the historical viaduct. The military characteristics of this bridge meant that only a small number of soldiers was needed to control those entering or leaving the town.

Alcántara Bridge. The Visigothic King Wamba carried out important defensive works in 674, which involved extending the walled enclosure and strengthening the bridge built by the Romans. In the days of Moorish dominion, Al-Mansur used the Roman and Visigothic structure of the bridge to extend it and make it impassable to any enemy wishing to enter the town. This contributed to giving Toledo its fame as an unconquerable stronghold. Alfonso VI's conquest of the town in 1085 was due to a well-planned strategy and a trick, which inspired Lope de Vega to write his comedy "*El hijo por engaño y toma de Toledo*." In the 13th century, during the reign of Alfonso X, "the Wise One", the bridge was reformed and rebuilt, emphasising its military function.

Bridges

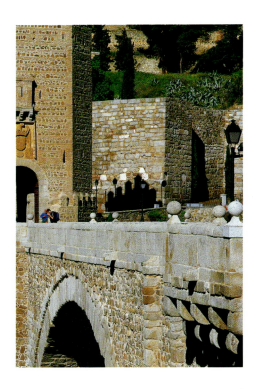

King Wamba Inscriptions. Until the 17th century, *Alcántara* Bridge, the oldest in Toledo, had a series of inscriptions on the walls of its hexagonal towers referring to dates of restoration. One of these inscriptions wrote how Wamba, in the 7th century, had restored its walls and those of the town, on top of which the Moors had put another inscription. In 1575, the *Corregidor* Juan Gutiérrez Tello removed these inscriptions and placed the ones referring to Wamba on one of the bridge towers.

Bridges

Water and Stone. The sharp bend of the Tagus around the granite hill and hillocks, popularly known as "el torno" ("the loop"), was probably why the *carpetanos* chose this emplacement for their primitive acropolis. And so a stronghold arose, which was so well-prepared for defence that, in time, it became encircled by walls and a crossing to which the Romans gave solid walls in order to resist the passing of the years. Then came the Moors who improved and strengthened it all.

Churches and Hospitals

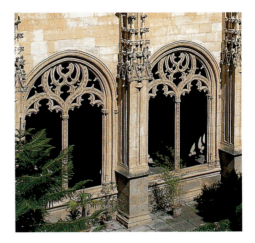

The Monastery of Victory. The Monastery of *San Juan de los Reyes* was built on the orders of Isabel I and Fernando of Aragón in order to commemorate their victory in the dynastic war begun by Juana of Castile, more known as *La Beltraneja*. It is a superb example of Gothic architecture, mainly carried out by Juan Guas, who finished its Isabelline structure in 1492. Its ribbed vaults are a fine example of a new and profoundly Christian European style of art.

Churches and Hospitals

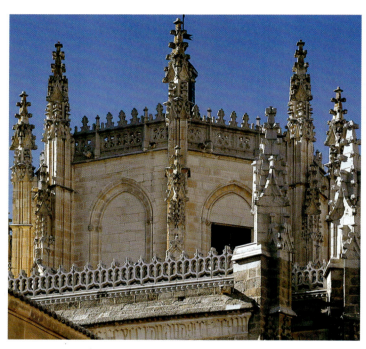

Nature and Imagination. During the reign of the Catholic Monarchs, Spanish Christianity found in the Gothic forms a way to express its relation with the European cultural tradition on the other side of the Pyrenees. Juan Guas, through his remarkable construction of *San Juan de los Reyes*, laid the foundations for the new spirit, blending imagination and Nature. So, spaces were opened up looking like geometrical and delicate forests of spiky ears of wheat, from where gargoyles, reading apes, stone martens, four-legged flying creatures and other elements peer out.

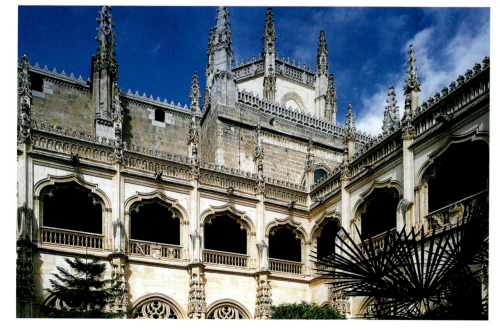

Churches and Hospitals

Isabelline Style. The Church of *San Juan de los Reyes* (left) is one of the most splendid examples of what was called the "Isabelline style". It is a version of the Flemish-Burgundinian Gothic style, lavishly interpreted through mudéjar art. The stellar-vaulted transept, the polygonal-shaped chapel and the adorning sculptures, well-represented in the Catholic Monarchs' coats-of-arms supported by eagles, are fine examples of the essential features of this style.

Gothic Splendour. The cloister of San Juan de los Reyes is a magnificent example of Gothic art in contact with the already declining mudéjar art. Its lavishly adorned sculptures repeat initials, coats-of-arms and symbols that refer to the Catholic Monarchs.

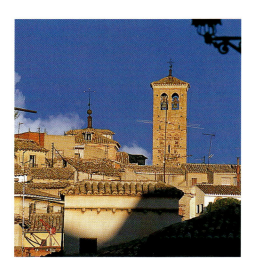

Santa Cruz Bell Tower. The old bell tower of the Church of Santa Cruz stands out high above the rooftops. Its sober and elegant lines blend in with the austere urban landscape of Christian Toledo.

Churches and Hospitals

Santa Cruz Patio. Enrique Egas, who started this building in 1504, built a splendid Greek cross temple, with various patios featuring double arcaded galleries and a magnificent staircase, the work of the maestro Alonso de Covarrubias, an example of the purest Plateresque style.

Santa Cruz Portal. This portal with touches of Gothic is by Alonso de Covarrubias around 1524. Beautiful features to be highlighted include the flat-arched doorway, with two windows almost joining at the top, and pairs of columns on either side.

Main Staircase. The same as the portal, the foot of the staircase that joins the main patio and the cloister is work of Covarrubias. The three different arches and their ornamentation remind us of the Florentine style.

Churches and Hospitals

Patio Galleries. Enrique Egas knew how to skilfully blend Gothic and mudéjar elements, as we can see in patios and arcaded galleries. His contribution was decisive for the consolidation of the transit toward Renaissance forms, just as we can observe in the columns.

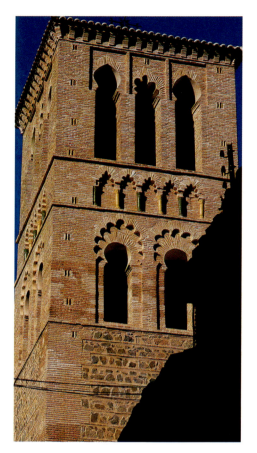

Tower of Santo Tomás. This is the church which houses El Greco's masterpiece "The Burial of the Count of Orgaz." The picture shows a miracle that occurred during the burial of Gonzalo Ruiz de Toledo, Chancellor of Castile and Lord of the town of Orgaz. Whilst the priest officiated beside the grave, St. Augustine and St. Stephen appeared and they themselves buried this holy man, who had given so much help to all those who had come to him.

Church of San Román. Superb mudéjar church which houses the Museum of Visigothic Culture and Councils. The dome and apse are by Alonso de Covarrubias and the magnificent retable is work of Diego Velasco. It is said that the site on which the church was built had formerly been the house of the martyr St. Leocadia.

Churches and Hospitals

Church of Santa Isabel. One of the most interesting aspects of architecture in Toledo is the blend of styles, which reflects the atmosphere of religious tolerance that existed in the city during centuries. Because of this mutual understanding among Christians, Muslims and Jews, Toledo became one of the most renowned Western centres of learning of the Middle Ages. The church walls bear witness to this fellowship of cultures.

Church of Santiago del Arrabal. The outer walls (right) show the brickwork peculiar to mudéjar art. It is a 13th –century Latin temple, but the oldest part dates from the previous century. One of the most attractive features of this religious monument is the harmonious blend of the old tower and the apse. The contrast of volumes responds to the Castilian idea of sturdiness and sobriety.

Church of Santa Leocadia. The only thing left of the old basilica is the mudéjar-style apse known today as *Cristo de la Vega* Hermitage. St. Leocadia died here around 304, victim of Emperor Diocletion's persecution. This church was built in the area known as *la Vega*, where, according to legend, Leocadia had been buried. In time, it became the church for Councils, of which various were held in the days of the Visigoths.

Churches

and Hospitals

Synagogues and Mosques

Arabs and Hebrews. The religious tolerance that prevailed for long periods of time made it possible for different communities to live together in harmony, which resulted in a very rich art full of details, reflecting various origins and stylistic ideas. The names, as well as the architectural forms and techniques of the *Tornerías* ("Turnery") and *Cristo de la Luz* ("Christ of the Light") mosques are proof of this.

Synagogues and Mosques

Synagogue of Santa María la Blanca. Built between the end of the 12th and beginning of the 13th centuries. It features five parallel aisles, whose wooden ceiling is supported by seven horseshoe arches on octagonal columns with tiled socles and capitals decorated in Persian-style stuccowork. Part of the ceiling of the main aisle is also covered with stuccos. The iris and the Star of David are the main ornamental motives of the Hebrew temple, which, apart from three later Christian chapels, practically remains unaltered since it was first built.

Synagogues and Mosques

The Nave of Yahvé. The sturdy columns and horseshoe arches with their fine ornamentation support the main aisle of *Santa María la Blanca*. In 1391, during a violent anti-Semite campaign by St. Vicente Ferrer, dozens of Jews were massacred here. A few years later, in 1405, the Hebrew temple was turned into a church. In 1550 Cardinal Silíceo dedicated it to a shelter for repentant women; from this time are also the three chapels at the current head of the building.

Mezquita de las Tornerías. This beautiful Muslim temple was erected in the 12th century, during the Christian period, as a sign of tolerance. Its thick columns and horseshoe arches built of brickwork distribute the layout of a square groundplan with truncated domes, through which white zenithal light shines.

Streets with History

Urban Poetics. Toledo is a city whose inhabitants have known how to develop urban poetry since ancient times. Every street, square, building, emblem or ornament talks to us not only of historical events, but also of a way of seeing life and a generous feeling that, for centuries, made living together in harmony and well-being possible among people of different cultures. This is why every street, like *Calle del Ángel*, seems to be a verse that evokes the true meaning of man and the direction of his destiny.

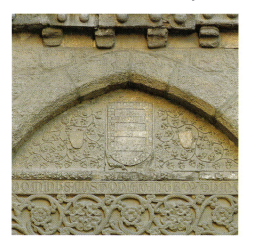

Streets with History

Love of Learning. Tradition marks the character of cities and its people. Toledo's tradition is marked by a love of learning, which reached its height in the Middle Ages with the *Escuela de Traductores* ("School of Translators"). Hence the fact that the scholar Marañón has a monument dedicated to him (right).

The Tranquillity of Everyday Life. The narrow streets of old Toledo lead out onto squares such as *Plaza de San Justo*. The townsfolk stroll leisurely beneath trees that await the season of budding, embracing that eternal feeling that means the prolongation of life and the experience of foreseeing the future in their offspring.

Streets with History

Plaza de Zocodover. This is the historical and commercial centre of Toledo. Its name comes from the Arabic word meaning "square of the beasts", but it is where all kinds of items were sold, as well as the place where bullfights and other popular events, such as the so-called *juegos de caña*, were held. Today it is surrounded by arcades and forged-iron balconies. From here, narrow streets lead to the Cathedral or to the Town Hall Square.

La Cuesta de la Reina. ("The Queen's Slope"). Neither Moors nor Christians could help avoid passing along these winding streets, whose narrowness seems to enhance the Gothic elegance of the Cathedral tower. However, the apparently chaotic layout of the town does have an explanation: it is due to the organisation of the town, where different communities, merchants and governors had their own territories.

Arches and Gates. The shaping of the town as a fortified enclosure led Romans, Visigoths, Moors and Christians to building walls with their corresponding gates and arches, such as the Moorish *Arco de la Sangre* ("Arch of Blood"). These gates and arches marked frontier spaces of chiaroscuros, meaning the difference between urban shelter and wild open countryside. From here, access was gained to the walled enclosure, whose primitive layout is attributed to Wamba, over the bridges of *Alcántara* and *San Martín*, and through the gates of *Bisagra Nueva*, *Alfonso VI* or *Bisagra Vieja*, *del Cristo de la Luz* or *Valmardón*, *Cambrón* or *Del Sol*.

Hillside Paths. From the *Paseo de San Cristóbal*, the streets seem to descend like hillside paths drawn by the rain. An enigmatic order appears to govern the directions that Toledans have memorised through time, needs and trades. Rooftops stretch up searching for the light, but only those of the temples reach out even higher, as if in this way the religious nature of a city that was imperial even before there was an empire was being established forever.

Streets with History

Streets with History

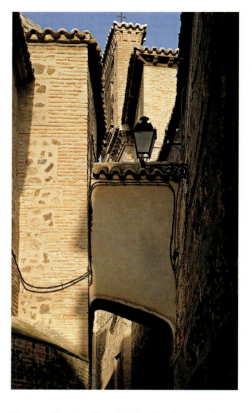

Calle del Ángel twists and turns, creating corners and chiaroscuros all the way along to the Monastery of *San Juan de los Reyes*.

Calle del Comercio. Main artery of the old and modern business centre of Toledo. At one end it joins up with the *Plaza de Zocodover*.

Travesía de Santa Isabel goes into the historic medieval city, where time seems to stand still between the walls of another age.

The District of Light. A thousand geometrical shining eyes seem to peer out toward the four cardinal points of the fertile plain, the river stretching between the *Alcázar* and the Cathedral.

Going towards the Plaza de Zocodover, Calle del Comercio appears to be haunted by shadows roaming between shop windows and billboards.

Swords and Marzipan

Arts and Crafts. The noble and metropolitan nature of Toledo made it a renowned industrial and business centre. Its inhabitants mastered many trades, but the city is especially famed for its marzipan, goldsmithery and silversmithery, where coats-of-arms and other symbols of heraldry referring to the many nobles living in the city, make up a good part of Toledan design.

Swords and Marzipan

Inns and Taverns were plentiful in Toledo, as authors such as Lope de Vega or Cervantes have pointed out on many an occasion. For example, *Las Pavas* is a famous one mentioned by Tirso de Molina. This long tradition carries on today in the form of mesones, those old-style taverns where succulent meals are dished up.

Crafts. Many are the shops which offer us typical food products, such as marzipan, olive oil and wine, but there are also many which sell items made by artisans, such as fine swords and damascene work.

Princes of Goldsmithery. Toledan goldsmiths and silversmiths, who have followed in the footsteps of the Moorish tradition, have been creating fine jewels and other ornamental items in gold and silver for centuries, which today fill shop windows and catch the eye of passers-by. These jewellers could well be given the name of the "princes of goldsmithery".

Swords and Marzipan

Skilled Masters. Between the 13th and 19th centuries, most of the Spanish goldsmiths and silversmiths, or those who worked in the Peninsula, were, directly or indirectly, related to the Toledan masters. The magnificence of the Processional Monstruance is not only explained by the talent and artistic sensibility of its author, Enrique de Arfe, but also by the atmosphere and richness of a city that attracted people who contributed their techniques and cultures.

Sensibility and Refinement. Two essential requirements for a goldsmith to carry out damascene work or *atauxia,* "Moorish craft of black steel inlaid with gold or silver", as Sebastián Covarrubias wrote.

SWORDS AND MARZIPAN | 93

Swords and Marzipan

Sweet Attraction. Though legend has it that marzipan was created in times of famine to ward off hunger, it reached its glory as an exquisite sweet on certain festivities, such as the Day of St. John [Midsummer Day], date on which Lope de Vega jokingly remarks how even nuns would fight to get some. Even Don Quixote has a weakness for this Toledan sweet of Moorish origin. Because, as Covarrubias states in his *Diccionario de Autoridades*, that "round cake" made of sugar and ground almonds is a "gift for the taste buds", unforgettable and filling.

The Charm of Old Toledo. This city remains faithful to its rich historical past. It is, as some chronicler has pointed out, a real inhabited museum, where ancient temples, churches, mosques or synagogues house and display their archaeological and historical treasures and paintings, etc., just like the Church of *Santo Tomé*, which houses one of the most important masterpieces in the history of Spanish painting, "The Burial of the Count of Orgaz", by El Greco. This is also true of the El Greco House and Museum, which still houses works by the Cretan and his disciples.

The Eye that Never Forgets. The stones in the walls have their ancient tales, their secret legends to tell, and the eye of the visitor, the eye that never forgets, retains the outside of the monuments, maybe the hustle and bustle of modern-day life that drowns out the whisper of the past; that obscure voice that may only be heard with the ears of sensitive souls.